SOUTH-WESTERN CAPE

4

of these families – the Bruniaceae. Fynbos is exceptional in that there are beautiful or interesting flowers to be found in it at any time of the year.

Veld fires are a regular occurrence in the fynbos and, in fact, are needed periodically to keep this vegetation type healthy. Many of the bulbous plants, like this watsonia, *Watsonia zeyheri* (1), flower *en masse* the season after a fire and provide an unforgettable spectacle. The large, nodding heads of the mountain dahlia, *Liparia splendens* (3), are seen at their best a few years after a fire; thereafter, the plants grow spindly and flower poorly.

Most phylicas have unimpressive flowers but the notable exceptions are the featherheads – *Phylica pubescens* (5) and the similar *Phylica plumosa*. In spring, when these plants flower profusely, their colour and texture are uniquely beautiful. In summer, the brilliant red flowers of the crassula, *Crassula coccinea* (4), show up dramatically against the sandstone rock of their mountain habitat. The grasshopper shown here is just a visitor – the flowers' red colour is in fact an advertisement for the Table Mountain pride butterfly.

5

• WILD FLOWERS •

FYNBOS

The protea family (Proteaceae) is one of the three plant families which characterise fynbos – another two are the Cape heaths (Ericaceae) and the Cape reeds (Restionaceae). The king protea, *Protea cynaroides* (7), is South Africa's national flower, and its huge flowerheads can open to more than 30 cm in diameter. The leaves surrounding the flowerheads of the geelbos, *Leucadendron salignum* (6) (which also belongs to the protea family), turn a brilliant yellow during the flowering season. The rooistompie, *Mimetes cucullatus* (10), another member of the protea family, here

WILD FLOWERS
OF SOUTHERN AFRICA

WILD FLOWERS

SOUTH-WESTERN CAPE

The south-western Cape is the heart of the Cape Floral Kingdom. To match the region's scenic splendour, a wide range of flowering plants grows naturally here, most of them found nowhere else in the world. Fynbos is the dominant vegetation type of the region and contains seven plant families which are confined to the Cape Flora. The rare rooistompie, *Brunia stokoei* (2), which grows in a small area of the coastal mountains near Betty's Bay, belongs to one

• SOUTH-WESTERN CAPE •

8

9

10

shows off its flowering colours against Cape reeds, *Elegia* sp.
   Brunsvigia marginata (8) superficially resembles the well-known Guernsey lily, *Nerine sarniensis* (which also originated from the south-western Cape), but is even more beautiful. The distinctively marked flowers of *Roella ciliata* (9) are a special feature of Cape fynbos in summer.

• WILD FLOWERS •

11

12

FYNBOS AND OTHER VELD TYPES

The Cape heaths (*Erica* spp.) belong to the Ericaceae family which also includes the heathers of Europe as well as azaleas and rhododendrons. Of the estimated 740 species found worldwide, astonishingly more than 640 are confined to the Cape Floral Kingdom. One of those, *Erica inflata* (11), provides a superb spectacle in the Groot Winterhoek wilderness area in summer.

One of the showiest and certainly the best known Cape orchid is the red disa, *Disa uniflora* (14), which flowers in summer along perennial mountain streams. *Phaenocoma*

SOUTH-WESTERN CAPE

13

14

15

prolifera (13) is one of many daisy plants called everlastings (because their flowers, if picked and dried, last indefinitely). In Afrikaans, they are called 'sewejaartjies' (little seven-year olds) because they flower most prolifically seven years after a fire.

Moraea neopavonia (12) is one of the peacock moraeas, so named because of the distinctive markings on the petals. Like most of the other peacock moraeas, it does not grow in fynbos but in another vegetation type, known as renosterveld, and like the other peacock moraeas, is very rare and endangered. The orange gazania, *Gazania krebsiana*, and lilac mesemb, *Drosanthemum hispidum* (15), grow together in yet another minor vegetation type of the Cape Flora – succulent karoo. Every year they contribute to the springtime flower spectacle between Worcester and Robertson.

• WILD FLOWERS •

WEST COAST

The Cape West Coast – the Atlantic seaboard south of the Olifants River and its hinterland – is a favourite springtime destination for flower lovers. Tourists visit the region's West Coast National Park to admire, among other things, the massed display of spring daisies on the granite hills above Langebaan lagoon (16). Granite also supports one of the most strikingly coloured mesembs, the goue vygie, *Lampranthus aureus* (20). Mesembs, ranging in colour from white to yellow through all shades of pink and lilac to deep red, and the annual daisies – white, orange, yellow, pink and blue – are the flowers mainly responsible for the large splashes of colour in the springtime landscape here.

Moraea calcicola (17), another peacock moraea, grows on limestone hills which are as much a feature of the West Coast as granite. It is another very rare plant,

WEST COAST

19

20

threatened by agriculture and urban expansion. *Nemesia versicolor* (19) which flowers in a variety of colour combinations, grows on the sandy flats of the West Coast. A species from the same genus, *Nemesia strumosa*, was used to produce the nemesia garden hybrids.

A few kilometres inland of the coast lies Darling – a town also known for its springtime display. The plants here grow on heavy clay soils and are quite different from those along the coast. The area is home to many spectacularly lovely bulbous plants, some of which are unique to Darling. These include the kelkiewyn (wine cup), *Geissorhiza radians* (18), here flowering with the white flowered chincherinchee, *Ornithogalum thyrsoides*, and the rose-pink and yellow satin flower, *Romulea eximia*.

• WILD FLOWERS •

21

23

22

NIEUWOUDTVILLE

Although not strictly part of Namaqualand, the area around Nieuwoudtville, on the Bokkeveld Escarpment, is often included in the itinerary of visitors who travel to Namaqualand to enjoy the spring flowers. And for good reason: in most years the springtime spectacle here is magnificent. Strictly speaking, the region's plants belong to the Cape Flora, and many are unique to the area. In Nieuwoudtville the annual spring show starts two to three weeks later than in most of Namaqualand, and continues into the early part of September.

But spring is not the only season when Nieuwoudtville puts on a floral display. In some years, during autumn, the mass flowering of the maartblom, Brunsvigia bosmaniae (21), on the dolerite koppies near the town can equal any spectacle offered later in the year. During the autumn months the river lilies, Crinum variabile (26), are also in flower. This is the only Crinum species found in the arid western part of southern Africa – all the others are

NAMAQUALAND

24

confined to well-watered habitats in the eastern parts of the region.

The other four flower species featured here are all part of Nieuwoudtville's spring display and are considered narrow endemics – they grow naturally only here. The orange bulbinella, *Bulbinella latifolia* var. *doleritica* (22), as its name suggests, is confined to dolerite koppies. The satin flower, *Romulea sabulosa* (24), grows in renosterveld on clay soils. So do *Sparaxis elegans* (23) and *Sparaxis tricolor* (25), the latter being one of Nieuwoudtville's special treasures, and a species which is exceptional in both colour and texture. These flowers are the source of the well-known sparaxis garden hybrids which are known and grown throughout the world.

• WILD FLOWERS •

28

NAMAQUALAND

Namaqualand is an arid region which receives most of its limited annual rainfall in winter. A vegetation type – known as succulent karoo – has evolved here which is as unique as the fynbos found further south. Many of Namaqualand's plants, like *Cephalophyllum spongiosum* (32) and the dwarf mesemb, *Conophytum meyeri* (30), have developed succulent stems or leaves which act as moisture reservoirs to enable them to survive the region's hot, desiccating summers. Succulent karoo vegetation also includes a great number of bulbous plants, such as the recently discovered *Babiana* sp. (29) and *Haemanthus coccineus* (28), whose underground parts survive the dry summers after their leaves and flowers have died off.

27

29

NAMAQUALAND

Annuals are another large group of Namaqualand flora. These plants survive the dry season in the form of seeds which germinate after the first autumn rains, and develop into plants which grow in winter, flower in spring and then die in summer.

Most people visit Namaqualand in spring to admire the mass flowering (27) of annuals like *Gazania lichtensteinii* (33) and *Heliophila schulzii* (31).

• WILD FLOWERS •

34

35

SUCCULENT KAROO

Aloes are found throughout southern Africa, in a variety of habitats. Many *Aloe* species have evolved succulent leaves and stems which enable them to meet the climatic demands of the subcontinent's arid regions. Namaqualand supports a number of these species, including *Aloe framesii* (34) featured here. Like aloes, mesembs are widespread, but it is in Namaqualand's succulent karoo vegetation that they have evolved a number of different forms to provide a wealth of species unmatched elsewhere in the region. Many of these forms are unique and very localised, like *Argyroderma fissum* (35) which is found only on quartz pebble patches on the Knersvlakte north and west of Vanrhynsdorp. The same is true of the dwarf mesemb, *Conophytum calculus* subsp. *calculus* (38). This species' flowers open up in the evening and are pollinated by moths.

NAMAQUALAND

In contrast to these localised species, the pale yellow flowers of *Grielum humifusum* (36) (shown here with a mesemb, *Cephalophyllum* sp.) are very common.

Many pelargoniums, like *Pelargonium echinatum* (37), have evolved fleshy stems which enable them to survive in the harsh environment of Namaqualand.

• WILD FLOWERS •

39

40

41

GARDEN ROUTE

Seduced by its magnificent scenery, its beaches and its gentle climate, it is easy to overlook the Garden Route's flowers. But this region was not named idly. It has a variety of habitats, ranging from the seashore over the coastal plateau to the Langeberg, Outeniqua and Tsitsikamma mountain ranges which run uninterrupted from the west to the east. Each of these has its own colourful collection of flowers.

It is here that southern Africa's greatest forests are found and, although in comparison with the fynbos and succulent karoo vegetation types they are not rich in species, they contain some of the subcontinent's most spectacular trees. One of these is the Cape chestnut, *Calodendrum capense* (39),

GARDEN ROUTE

42

43

which in full summer flower stands out against the rich green of the forest canopy. It may (or may not!) surprise readers to learn that this plant belongs to the same family as citrus (Rutaceae).

In the fynbos, which grows on the wet southern slopes of the Garden Route mountains, many ericas can be found – some have flowers which are lovely individually, like *Erica versicolor* (41), others, like *Erica melanthera* (40), are striking when they flower *en masse*. This habitat is also home to one of the Cape Flora's most beautiful gladioli, *Gladiolus sempervirens* (42), which flowers in summer and is pollinated by the Table Mountain pride butterfly, *Aeropetes tulbaghia*.

Gazania rigens (43) grows on the coastal rocks right next to the sea. It is one of the few plants that can survive the constant salt sea-spray which would kill most other plants.

• WILD FLOWERS •

45

44

FORESTS AND MOUNTAINS

Unlike the south-western Cape, where the summers are dry, the Garden Route enjoys rain all year round, but with slightly greater falls in autumn and spring. This is the reason why large tracts of natural forest are found here whereas, further west, forests are confined to small patches on wet mountain slopes and kloofs. On the forest margins grow a number of flowering shrubs, like the four corners bush, *Grewia occidentalis* (47). The lichens growing on the branches are typical of this moist habitat. Also growing next to the forest are wild dagga plants, *Leonotis leonurus* (45), their tubular orange flowers a favoured source of nectar for the greater double-collared sunbird which is often seen in this environment.

GARDEN ROUTE

The southern slopes of the Outeniqua mountains are home to one of the fynbos's most extraordinary daisy plants. The strawberry everlasting, *Syncarpha eximia* (46), carries a head of pink flowers which open to a brilliant orange on a long (up to 2 m), generally unbranched stem. On these same slopes, after a veld fire, the George (or Knysna) lily, *Cyranthus elatus* (44), flowers in its thousands to provide an unforgettable sight. These magnificent flowers are also sometimes seen in forest clearings or on their fringes.

Ceratandra grandiflora (48) is an orchid which grows in the tall, dense fynbos of the Garden Route's coastal plateau.

• WILD FLOWERS •

49

50

51

EASTERN CAPE

The best-known flower from the Eastern Cape is the crane flower, *Strelitzia reginae* (55). Its natural habitat is a thicket type of vegetation called valley bushveld – unique to the Eastern Cape – where the popular garden shrub, plumbago *Plumbago auriculata* (50), also grows.

Another garden favourite is the Cape honeysuckle, *Tecomaria capensis* (51), which grows naturally on scrub forest margins – also

• EASTERN CAPE •

52

53

54

the habitat of the amatungulu, *Carissa macrocarpa* (53), which produces its sweetly scented flowers in summer and its scarlet fruits in autumn.

The pom-pom tree, *Dais cotinifolia* (52), is a large shrub or small tree found in wooded kloofs where it flowers vividly, but briefly, in summer. The lucky bean tree, *Erythrina lysistemon* (54), on the other hand, grows in isolation on hillsides. Grasslands are where *Kniphofia linearifolia* (49), one of the red-hot pokers, produces its flowers in summer to attract its pollinator, the Table Mountain pride butterfly, *Aeropetes tulbaghia*.

55

• WILD FLOWERS •

KWAZULU-NATAL

The highest mountain peak in Africa south of Kilimanjaro is Thaba Ntlenyana (3 482 m) which is part of the high plateau in Lesotho whose eastern escarpment forms the mighty KwaZulu-Natal Drakensberg range. These towering cliffs are made of basalt, a rock of volcanic origin on which grows one of the 'Berg's loveliest bulbous plants, *Rhodohypoxis baurii* (58). The basalt

KWAZULU-NATAL

59

60

61

overlies a softer rock, cave sandstone, which erodes more easily to form the more gentle contours of the Drakensberg's lower slopes. *Protea caffra* (56) is one of the two common large proteas which dot these grassy slopes (the other is *Protea roupelliae*). One of several everlastings found in the Drakensberg is *Helichrysum adenocarpum* (61).

At lower altitudes in the KwaZulu-Natal midlands, a rare plant, one of the pincushions in the protea family (Proteaceae), *Leucospermum gerrardii* (60), can be found growing in open grasslands on outcroppings of Table Mountain sandstone. *Cyrtanthus galpinii* (59) flowers in autumn along river banks. One of several hibiscuses found in KwaZulu-Natal, *Hibiscus aethiopicus* (57), is a low-growing perennial with soft stems which sprout from a permanent woodstock after the frequent fires in its grassland habitat.

• WILD FLOWERS •

DRAKENSBERG

The grass-covered hills of the KwaZulu-Natal midlands and the slopes of the lower Drakensberg support a variety of lovely bulbous plants. One of these is *Hesperantha scopulosa* (63). Others are the elegant hair-bells, *Dierama* spp. (65) which, when not in flower, resemble clumps of grass. The best known is the flame lily, *Gloriosa superba* (62). Two of KwaZulu-Natal's loveliest bulbs carry the same

• KWAZULU-NATAL •

65

66

common name, Christmas bells, and also look quite similar. Both grow on the fringes of riverine forest as climbers on the surrounding vegetation. *Littonia modesta* (64) has nodding open flowers whereas *Sandersonia aurantiaca* (66) produces hanging flowers shaped like Chinese lanterns.

• WILD FLOWERS •

68

69

67

HIGHVELD

The highveld of South Africa's Gauteng, Mpumalanga and Northern provinces is, in broad terms, a high plateau of rolling hills bordered in the east by a north-south lying range of mountains which includes the northern Drakensberg (distinct from but in line with the KwaZulu-Natal Drakensberg), and the Makonjwa and Wolkberg ranges. To the east and north-east, this range drops steeply into the lowveld. Most of the highveld is covered with grassland but there are patches of forest on the mountains and on the escarpment edge. These patches are the habitat of the wild gardenia, *Rothmannia capensis* (71), a shrub which produces its fragrant flowers in summer.

The Mickey Mouse bush, *Ochna natalitia* (68), takes its name from the dark red-black fruits attached to a receptacle with bright red sepals which resemble the large ears of Disney's cartoon character. The small yellow flowers are produced in spring. The wild fox-glove, *Ceratotheca triloba* (67), is a soft shrublet with particularly lovely delicate pink flowers whose outer petals, like the new leaves and buds, are

HIGHVELD

densely covered with soft fine hairs. This plant, like *Gladiolus dalenii* (69), favours open grassland. The most brilliantly coloured of several highveld gladioli, *G. dalenii* was probably one of the southern African species used to produce the hybrid gladioli which are now cultivated all over the world.

The yellow arum, *Zantedeschia pentlandii* (70), is a very rare plant also found in grassland on rocks and next to streams. This is one of the South African species of arums that has been used by New Zealand plant breeders to produce a range of spectacularly coloured garden hybrids. One of the other species was *Z. rehmanii*, the pink arum which is found in the southern escarpment.

The Barberton daisy, *Gerbera jamesonii* (72), is well known to gardeners in the form of a variety of cultivars. The original Barberton daisy grows wild in shady spots on the escarpment.

• WILD FLOWERS •

73

74

LOWVELD

The lowveld of South Africa's Mpumalanga and Northern provinces includes one of southern Africa's most popular tourist attractions, the Kruger National Park. Since most visitors to South Africa make this one of their destinations, many will be familiar with at least some of the region's botanical splendours. The lowveld is dominated by a wealth of different trees. Many of these are spectacular when in flower, like the wild pear, *Dombeya rotundifolia* (76).

• LOWVELD •

75

76

77

Anybody who visits the Kruger Park in winter will be impressed by the impala lily, *Adenium multiflorum* (75), in flower. It is a member of the Apocynaceae family which includes other succulent-stemmed plants from arid regions.

Pride-of-De-Kaap, *Bauhinia galpinii* (77), grows naturally in riverine thickets and can reach a diameter of 4–5 m. Also found here is the flame creeper, *Combretum microphyllum* (73). In spring, this vigorous creeper is coloured scarlet by its profusion of flowers. The spreading wild morning glory, *Ipomoea crassipes* (74), trails sheets of deep pink flowers in summer.

WILD FLOWERS

ZIMBABWE

Bordering Mozambique, Zimbabwe's Eastern Highlands are traversed by several mountain ranges. Of these, the Chimanimani Mountains are unique and of considerable botanical interest. The quartzitic rock of these mountains carries a vegetation which is strikingly similar to the Cape's fynbos, and which includes members of the Cape reed family, Restionaceae, as well as ericas. The pincushion, *Leucospermum saxosum* (78), is a typical example of the plants found in this habitat. Further north lies Mt. Inyangani, the highest point in Zimbabwe. After one of the frequent fires known to occur in this region, *Cyrtanthus breviflorus* (82) flowers in profusion in a swamp on its summit ridge. *Gladiolus melleri* (81) also flowers after fires but is found on the western approaches to the Eastern Highlands.

ZIMBABWE

80

81

82

83

The black-eyed susan, *Thunbergia alata* (79), is a soft-stemmed creeper which shrouds trees on the margins of tropical forest. The water lily, *Nymphaea nouchali* (80), can be found in perennial standing water. This plant, with its exquisite blue to mauve flowers, is a true African cosmopolitan, found literally from the Cape to Cairo. An otherwise insignificant shrub, *Rhigozum zambesiacum* (83), bursts into brilliant yellow flower in its lowveld habitat in spring.

WILD FLOWERS

84

NAMIBIA

Namibia is a fascinating country with vast expanses of arid land, including one of the world's oldest deserts, the Namib. Some of the country's most interesting plants are found in these dry areas. *Pachypodium lealii* (85), a large, succulent-stemmed plant, here shown growing in Damaraland, is endemic to Namibia.

The quiver-tree, *Aloe dichotoma* (86), is found in Namibia's dry southern parts as well as in Namaqualand and Bushmanland south of the Orange River. Its name dates back to the times when Khoi-San hunters used its hollowed out branches for storing poisoned arrows. One of the region's carrion flowers, *Hoodia gordonii* (84), has a similar distribution. Its flowers give off a potent stench, similar to that of rotting meat, to attract the blowflies which pollinate them.

85

INDABA PUBLISHING

ISBN 1-86872-192-2